I0044801

CRACKING

5 MYTHS OF STARTING

THE

OR GROWING A

START-UP

SMALL BUSINESS

CODE

SAM CIBRONE

THE SMALL BUSINESS MYTHBUSTER

INDIE BOOKS
INTERNATIONAL®

ISBN: 978-1-952233-48-7
Library of Congress Control Number: 2020918914

McPherson, mcphersongraphics.com

INDIE BOOKS INTERNATIONAL, INC®
2424 VISTA WAY, SUITE 316
OCEANSIDE, CA 92054

www.indiebooksintl.com

I would like to dedicate this book to my lovely wife, Jenn, my wonderful son, Noah, and to my precious daughter, Ella, for their support. It has been the key to my life. Thank you, Family.

MEET THE MYTHS

- (**M**) The **M**oney Myth
- (**Y**) The **Y**ou Myth
- (**T**) The **T**reatment Myth
- (**H**) The **H**ow Myth
- (**S**) The **S**pending Myth

CONTENTS

PART I

WHY BUILDING A BUSINESS FOR GROWTH MATTERS

CHAPTER ONE

WHY YOU SHOULD NOT TRUST BUSINESS MYTHS

There are many books about starting a business, but most of them do not focus on creating the right mindset; they usually jump right into the process. This book is different since it focuses on five myths of starting a small business. By debunking these myths, a mindset of confidence, determination, and strength will be created that will allow you to implement the process of successfully starting a small business. Next, I will help you focus on the nuts and bolts of getting the business started. Then, I want to assist you by focusing on sustaining growth.

BY DEBUNKING THESE MYTHS, A MINDSET OF CONFIDENCE, DETERMINATION, AND STRENGTH IS CREATED THAT ALLOWS YOU TO IMPLEMENT THE PROCESS OF SUCCESSFULLY STARTING A SMALL BUSINESS.

In this immediate society, people want to know the basic steps to achieve a solution. For example, if you want to know how to select a career, there is a step-by-step process that starts with identifying your interest or passion. Another view would be to start with what Tom Rath says in his book *Life's Greatest Question*: "Where can I find my greatest contribution?" These conflicting viewpoints are both a possible step one in choosing a career.

The second step would be to take some kind of assessment to define your strengths and weaknesses. The steps in this process go on until you have your career formula. There is nothing wrong with step-by-step processes to help you be effective in accomplishing your goals; in fact, our society has progressed so fast that through technology, we can learn how to do things almost instantly—sharing information to attack problems or find solutions through processes via YouTube, Facebook, and other tools. Tony Robbins and Dean Grazioso have fine-tuned a concept called Masterminds—courses that can be developed by anyone who has expertise in something. This allows you to learn processes, concepts, and information much faster, as you do not spend time in trial and error. You learn from someone who has successfully done what you are trying to accomplish. In addition, taking courses involves people who share a desire to help solve each other's problems related to the topic. In this case, the Mastermind would be "How to Select a Career," hosted by someone with expertise in doing that. Attendees could all contribute and help each other select careers. It is predicted that knowledge-based businesses like Masterminds will soon be a billion-dollar industry.

Process books are great for helping you with the step-by-step implementation of ideas. There are many experts who believe we need to focus on mindset first. For example, Simon Sinek wrote a book called *What is Your Why?* His basic premise is that we must understand why before we do anything. I did not just learn this concept from books; I lived it. While creating my Mastermind course, "How to Start a Business," I learned if you do not create a clear mindset, you will never build a great Mastermind course. Before I developed my course, I took Module One of the online course, "Mastering Your Mindset." In that module, I learned I had to avoid the negativity of others, be confident and determined, use transformational vocabulary, and realize my why. The epiphany that came from this was that life is not about me; it is about adding value to others. It also became clear we must create our mindset first to ensure a successful start-up and grow a business.

I surveyed many people who wanted to start a small business about what was holding them back and found 90 percent of the responses had something to do with fear. That included fear of the unknown, failure, potential loss of money, lack of resources, incompetency, enormous workload, and the list goes on and on. I wrote this book for these people—and anyone else who's allowed the five myths of starting or growing a small business to stop them from moving forward. You will gain confidence and be ready to act after debunking these myths. Then, I will give you ways to build your future business and sustain growth.

CHAPTER TWO

HOW TO GROW ANY SMALL BUSINESS: MY MESS TO SUCCESS

T o understand my work, I think you need to know my personal background, which created my mindset. I was born in the Steel City—Pittsburgh, Pennsylvania—in 1971, when the steel mills were flourishing. I came from a low-income family; my mother and father worked diligently just to put food on the table. Almost everyone we knew in the neighborhood were hard-working blue-collar people.

Hard, manual work is the best as it shows character was ingrained into my mind while growing up. I was taught that I would work for someone or in some company. There were no entrepreneurs in my neighborhood, nor did we have any friends or relatives who were entrepreneurs, unless you count my uncle Mike, who fixed the cars of friends and family. Being a blue-collar worker was a way to be part of our community.

How did I change my mindset from one that said I could never start a business to becoming an entrepreneur? I started with small successes that led to massive growth. From a young age, I watched my family and friends work for others, and I decided I would work for myself one day. I wanted to be my own boss. I knew if I worked more earnestly and religiously than other people, I could be successful. As a result, I was always trying to improve a little each day. A perfect example of this philosophy was explained to me by my current neighbor, Dean Minuto, author of the book *Yescalator*. He reminded me, "If you get 1 percent better every day, that is over a 300 percent improvement in a year." When I look back, I realize that graduating from high school, going away to college, and getting a master's degree were all impactful to my mindset. After all, I was the only one in my family to do those three things. These steps made me realize that I needed to have a mindset of confidence—that *I*

HOW DID I CHANGE MY MINDSET FROM ONE THAT SAID I COULD NEVER START A BUSINESS TO BECOMING AN ENTREPRENEUR? I STARTED WITH SMALL SUCCESSES THAT LED TO MASSIVE GROWTH.

can accomplish things through hard work. I did not have a high IQ, but I did have a strong work ethic. I genuinely believed in this philosophy. In fact, when I took my first teaching job in Tampa, Florida, in 1995, the message on my bulletin board was, "Learning is based on *I will* not IQ!"

I taught students with learning disabilities at middle school and high school for five years and emphasized to them that their hard work would lead to success. Teaching was a great profession—I was extremely happy about the impact I was making on young students. However, I wanted supplemental income, so I had to address the five myths I had grown up hearing before I could launch my first business. So, I kept within my comfort zone and decided to work for someone else at a tutoring center. However, the lightbulb finally went on as I realized in working there, I was what the center was getting paid for—*my* tutoring. I decided to develop a business plan after learning how the center ran its business. I continued to work there for three months and examine my future competitor. Then, I launched my own business, called Tampa Tutoring. It was a huge success, but you will learn about that later.

IN FACT, WHEN I TOOK MY FIRST TEACHING JOB IN TAMPA, FLORIDA, IN 1995, THE MESSAGE ON MY BULLETIN BOARD WAS, "LEARNING IS BASED ON I WILL NOT IQ!"

Three years later, I was approached by five players on my high school's volleyball team to start a volleyball club for kids. Initially, I listened to that doubtful voice in my head saying, *You know nothing about volleyball clubs,* so I declined. However, my players were persistent, so I made a deal with them that if they could find me a roster of ten players, I would start a club. I started a small one-team club and later merged with two others to become Tampa United Volleyball Academy, which is still in existence over twenty years later. This business continues to thrive because my partner Gary and I have always stuck to our values.

Fast-forward to today: I have owned five successful small businesses. In fact, I currently still own three of them and have kept my full-time college coaching job for most of the time. Currently, the three businesses require a minimal amount of time from me because I was able to empower great people to manage them. Like Jim Collins, author of *Good to Great*, said, "If you have the right people on the bus and in the right seat, your company will be successful." Since I have time on my hands, I started another business this year, Sam Cibrone

Business Coaching, where I help others start or grow their businesses. I decided to combine the skills learned through twenty-five years of athletic coaching and twenty-three years of owning businesses to help others grow their businesses. It was only appropriate for me to use both strengths to make an impact on other people's lives.

If I had let the five business growth myths control my mindset, I would not have started any of my small businesses. I would be nearing my twenty-fifth teaching anniversary, earning a salary of about $60,000 per year. Even though I loved teaching in the classroom, I make about four times that salary now, teach business, mentor, and still impact lives. Most importantly, I have a great relationship with God; my wife, Jenn; my son, Noah; and my daughter, Ella— because as a business owner, I can create more time for what matters most.

PART II

BUSTING THE FIVE BUSINESS GROWTH MYTHS

CHAPTER THREE

MYTH 1: **THE MONEY MYTH**

IT TAKES MONEY TO MAKE MONEY

A s I was growing up, I was constantly told you must have money to make money. However, I eventually learned that is a myth. I learned you need to be resourceful with start-up costs, maintain a source of income, and provide great customer service to be a successful business owner. If you focus on this, money is not your deciding factor. Here are two short stories from my personal life that changed my opinion and made me realize it is a myth that it takes money to make money.

I LEARNED YOU NEED TO BE RESOURCEFUL WITH START-UP COSTS, MAINTAIN A SOURCE OF INCOME, AND PROVIDE GREAT CUSTOMER SERVICE TO BE A SUCCESSFUL BUSINESS OWNER.

The first story that opened my eyes was in my first business, Tampa Tutoring. In the fall of 1995, I began my second year of teaching middle school. I loved my job because I was able to help special education children. At that time, my girlfriend and I were dreaming of marriage and a family. However, I chose a great profession that paid poorly. My teaching salary was a whopping $23,000 a year, with only a 3-percent raise each year. I was very discouraged, as I knew I could not raise a family on that salary. My girlfriend was a teacher, too, but I wanted her to be able to stay home if she wanted as a mom. It would be exceedingly difficult to raise a family on a single teaching salary. So, I began to realize I needed a new job or some supplemental income. One of the teachers at my school told me about a tutoring opportunity at Sylvan Learning Center. I was offered an extra $400 per month, but I proudly declined as I had a master's in special education. They countered with $600 a month for twelve hours a week. I was not extremely happy, but I accepted the position since I needed the money.

One month went by, and I concluded that I enjoyed tutoring; it was a personal way of teaching for me. Since I liked it so much, I was hoping it could be my way to earn a solid extra income. However, I reexamined my budget and came to the realization that an extra $600 a month would not allow me to support the family I planned on having. Being a lifelong learner was always a passion of mine, so I observed Sylvan Learning Center's business model. I came to understand that my *service* was really the most important aspect of the business. Consequently, I realized if I provided a great tutoring experience with high academic results, I could have my own business.

As a result, I decided I needed to start my own business and wrote a business plan to make an additional $80,000 a year. I felt this income could be achieved based on my former employer's income figures, and it would provide the lifestyle I wanted for my family. Just like most people, my excitement and apprehensions were equally strong. I knew Tampa Tutoring would not be easy, so my first lesson was the need to be incredibly careful with start-up costs. I started with only $1,000 and spent it on a security deposit and my first month's rent for office space. I got free teaching resources from a book depository that recycled old books. I even asked friends for used supplies since most of them were teachers, too. I took the answering machine from my house and put it in the office to avoid purchasing one. Another way I tried to be resourceful was to put multiple students in each tutoring room. This was a total failure, as the customers needed their own rooms to thrive and learn. So, I had to adjust and enforce a limit of one student per room. Despite my failure, I decided to push forward. I remembered a valuable lesson learned when I was a student-athlete: do not give up when faced with obstacles. Perseverance leads to success.

The second lesson I learned was that I needed to keep earning a steady income when starting a small business. I got lucky with this one because I did not want to quit teaching. The problem people run into when starting a business is that they want to go all-in, but are not able to deal with living expenses because it takes time to build profit. The fact that I continued to teach allowed me to live off that salary while I was acquiring clients and improving the product.

The third lesson I learned is that it is not about price or making money. You must deliver great

THE SECOND LESSON I LEARNED WAS THAT I NEEDED TO KEEP EARNING A STEADY INCOME WHEN STARTING A SMALL BUSINESS.

customer service to eliminate price concerns and generate revenue quickly. You also must provide a great product from the very beginning of your business. I made two mistakes in this area. As stated earlier, I put two students in each tutoring room, which negatively affected their experience. The other mistake was that I only offered teachers two dollars more than what they were making at my competitor's tutoring center. I know we needed great teachers, but this was not enough to recruit a teacher to leave an established business. So, I increased their pay to recruit great teachers to solve that problem. Immediately, customer service improved.

From my failures, I learned some valuable lessons. First, I could not sacrifice customer service to save on costs. It was better to have one person per room, which was less efficient but of better quality. Second, I needed to pay the teachers fifteen dollars per hour, as they received ten dollars at the other learning centers, and a 33-percent increase was significant enough to recruit them to my business. The three lessons—resourcefully limiting start-up costs, maintaining an income, and providing great customer service—developed a recipe for success. All the tutoring rooms were occupied, and we were turning clients away. Then, the real epiphany came to me—I could own a business and profit from it without being there. This excited me, as I started to understand entrepreneurship. The concept of working *on* my business instead of *in* my business became apparent. In fact, I could just tutor when I wanted to because I enjoyed it, and when I did, I received the full revenue. The challenge was not to be a great tutor but to get great people who could do the job as well as I could, if not better. Months later, it was time to make my profit-and-loss statement; my gross profit was over $80,000. I reached my goal of earning a salary that would support my future family.

Two years later, the tutoring business was running great; my students saw huge improvements in their grades, reading levels, standardized test scores, and project scores. In addition, my clientele was increasing through referrals and marketing. People felt they were receiving great tutoring with a more personal connection. I was making a great salary with my supplemental income, and I still got to do what I loved—teach.

I STARTED TO UNDERSTAND ENTREPRENEURSHIP. THE CONCEPT OF WORKING ON MY BUSINESS INSTEAD OF IN MY BUSINESS BECAME APPARENT.

The moral of the story: you do not have to have a lot of money to launch a service business. It does not take much to earn money in a service business; I started Tampa Tutoring with $1,000. It takes being creative with start-up costs, having another source of income when you begin, and producing a great service at an affordable price. Do this, and your early clients will help you grow your business by referrals. Then, maintain great service, and you will have a great business.

In the second story, I mentored my wife as she started her business. Once again, I discovered it is not necessary to have a lot of money to make money when I consulted on my wife's business, Pura Vida Volleyball. The first two lessons I learned from Tampa Tutoring—be resourceful with initial costs and maintain an income— were appropriate here, but there was a new third lesson: plan strategically.

In 2011, my wife, Jenn, was terribly busy. She was finishing her MBA, pregnant with our first child, and promoted to national account manager in her corporate job. The promotion brought our family a huge pay increase, with Jenn earning a substantial income. In the midst of this chaos,

Jenn came to me with two realizations: she was not happy in corporate America, and she wanted to start her own business. We sat down and discussed the options. She explained her passions were volleyball and fashion design, so she wanted to start a retail volleyball apparel company.

Jenn knew she would have a crazy life—she was going to have a baby, wanted to finish her MBA, maintain her national account manager job, and grow Pura Vida Volleyball. She set an ambitious goal to earn enough from Pura Vida so she could leave corporate America. She would need to gross at least triple her current salary to achieve that.

The first question I asked her was how much it would cost to start the business. She stated the initial investment was only $5,000. My next consulting question: how could she be resourceful with her initial costs? She explained she was only going to sell tournament t-shirts— the most purchased item—to maximize profit and minimize inventory. Second, she was only going to buy one silk screen machine. Finally, she would start with no staff, press the shirts herself, and fulfill orders with some shirts we already had completed. These three adjustments allowed Jenn to minimize initial costs.

The second way to start a business without lots of money is to not pay yourself a salary immediately. As a previous owner of two small businesses and the current owner of two other businesses, I suggested she start the business while keeping her full-time job.

The third lesson I taught Jenn was that strategic planning was the key to starting a business without lots of overhead. She had never owned a business before and never worked in retail. So, she limited costs with careful product selection and low inventory. She did not want to waste money on products that might not sell. Also, she was very strategic in what events she wanted to attend. She started with my two local tournaments, so there were no travel costs and low vendor fees, and she was remarkably familiar with these events. Another strategy she decided to try was online sales; it requires little overhead to build an online store, but requires a lot of set-up time. This was a total failure because the main reason for purchasing a T-shirt at an event is because you are *at the event*, so she did not get many orders online. She had limited time to put any additional work into the online store, but Jenn discovered event-goers were her ideal customers, not online shoppers.

The last strategic initiative was to be a secondary vendor at the volleyball tournaments. This meant she could only sell items the main vendor did not sell—so she did not get to sell tournament t-shirts. Hence, this idea was another failure because she did not generate enough sales to cover her costs. She needed to choose her events more carefully.

The experience taught Jenn many things about her business. First, she needed to be resourceful with low initial costs. Second, she needed to have another source of income. Third, she needed to have a strategic plan on inventory and which events to choose. Three years went by extremely fast, and Jenn was elated to find she had met her goals for gross revenue and profit. Jenn had found her recipe for making Pura Vida Volleyball a success.

Fast-forwarding eight years to 2019, Jenn improved her business and became the main tournament merchandiser for seventeen strategically selected events from Boston to Tampa. In 2011, her largest event was 200 teams, but in 2019 in Boston, she serviced over 1,000 teams. Her gross budget has quadrupled; she is the largest mobile volleyball event merchandiser in Florida.

Once again, what is the moral of the story? Jenn took $5,000 and created a business that has increased her salary to three times her corporate America income by 2020. It is a myth that it takes money to make money, even for a retail business. It takes resourcefulness with initial costs. It takes keeping a revenue stream that allows you to grow the business slowly without the stress of supporting yourself. Finally, it takes strategic planning to attend the right events to maximize profit and achieve efficiency. These three things were the recipe for success in starting a business without a lot of money.

APPLICATION BOX

1. List your top ten initial costs, then prioritize them.

2. List the three mandatory expenses and how you will resourcefully cut costs.

3. Explain how you will acquire income while slowly growing your business.

4. List three ways your customer service will be better than other companies.

5. Explain the key elements in your strategic plan.

CHAPTER FOUR

MYTH 2: **THE YOU MYTH**

YOU ARE YOUR SMALL BUSINESS

nother myth in starting or growing a small business is based on a skewed view. *You are your small business.* This is a myth because your business has so many factors that identify it. You are only a small part of your business. Here are a couple of short stories that debunk the myth that you are the center of your business.

In my first year of high school coaching, I was asked to start a volleyball club. Club Tampa Volleyball began as a one-team club with me as the head coach. By the third year, I had eight

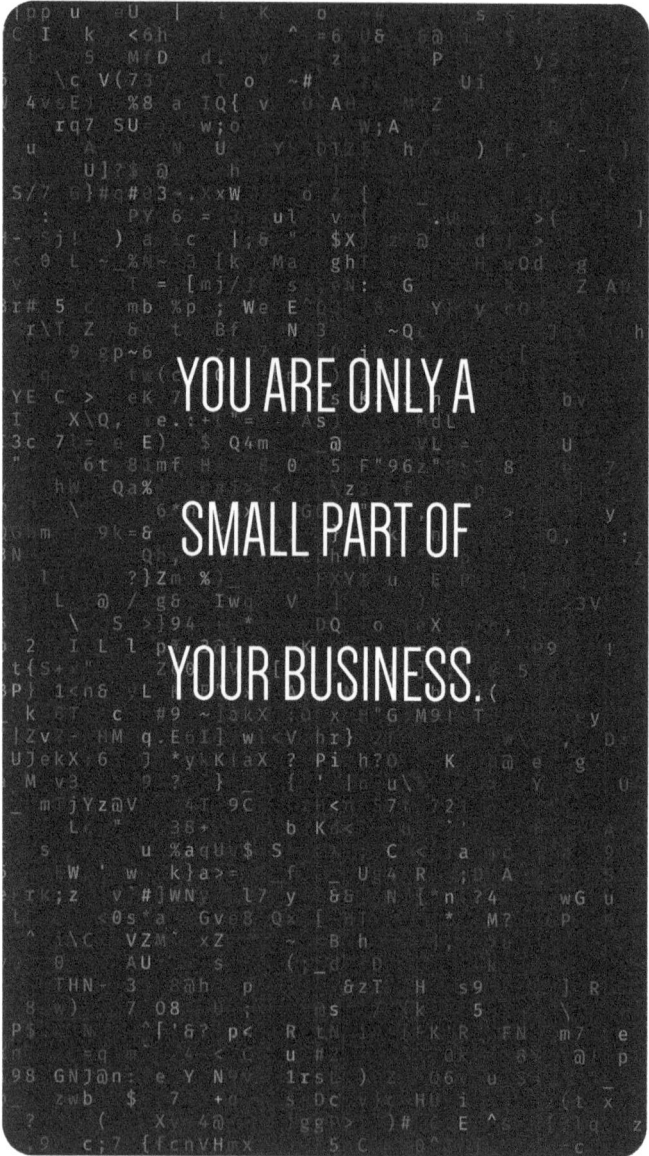

YOU ARE ONLY A SMALL PART OF YOUR BUSINESS.

teams in the club. My current partner, Gary, was on a similar road; he started at the same time and had progressed to an eleven-team club called Sandspurs Volleyball Club. We, young coaches, were helping the youth of Tampa Bay, teaching them life lessons through sports, and getting them college scholarships.

As Club Tampa and Sandspurs grew, Gary and I came to some realizations. Both clubs outgrew their current facility, and we were challenged with finding great coaches because most wanted to coach the elite club and compete at a higher level. In addition, a lot of the top athletes were already at the elite club, and neither of us could afford to lose good athletes.

In the summer after our third season, Gary and I decided to meet to talk about our clubs. We both believed the myth that we *were* our businesses and agreed that retention, quality coaches, and facilities were problems we both had. So, we decided to merge our organization and keep Gary's business name, the Sandspurs Volleyball Club. I was fine with it since Club Tampa sounded like a nightclub, anyway. At first, this merger was a difficult concept for both of us; since we believed *we* were our companies, we were afraid it would affect our ability to keep the business the way we had it before. Luckily, we had the same goals of quality coaching, a family-centered atmosphere at our own facilities, and retaining at least 70 percent of our clients and coaches.

The merger began. We rented a big facility for our twenty-five-team club, and all the teams trained under one roof. To achieve the goals of quality coaching and retention, Gary and I decided to write all the practice plans for each age group and vary them based on their skill level. This was a huge failure because the coaches felt we did not think they were good at coaching. As a result, our retention rate was only 60 percent.

Gary and I met to discuss the issue, and we quickly realized we did not execute the plan properly. We needed to explain to the coaches and players our purpose behind the training style. For example, the plans were written to give accountability to our training and enhance their coaching opportunities. In fact, the coaches were allowed the freedom to modify drills for their team's weaknesses. The players needed to know this was not to make volleyball boring but to create efficiency since we only trained two days a week.

Later, another obstacle appeared. A new club opened that was paying coaches two to four times what we paid. It also let many players play for free to get the best talent. The owner was a multimillionaire, so profitability and being the biggest club in the country were not as crucial to his success. We quickly saw some of our coaches and players defect to the new club.

Once again, we had to focus on relationships with our coaches and players to retain them. Gary and I met with the coaches, players, and parents to assure our dedication to them. In fact, many other clubs were bought out by the new club, but we refused to sell and maintained our family atmosphere. Due to this situation, our club shrank from twenty-five to eleven teams, but we still had great coaches and good players.

After five years of the new club, we knew we had weathered the storm. Our team numbers were about the same each year; we even turned away some players to maintain our size. Then, it was the end of our fifth season of the new club's domination. Gary and I had our end-of-the-year meeting. We looked at our retention rate, and it was 75 percent. We had surpassed our goal of 70 percent by providing great coaching. In addition, our coaching staff retention rate was 95 percent, which was amazing.

Fast-forward to 2019, when we were the longest-surviving club in Tampa, going into its twenty-first season. We have sent more kids to college than any other club in Tampa. We have the best players and coach retention rate in Tampa. So, what is the moral of the story? It is a myth that *you* are your business. Gary and I were not the club. We learned that our coaches, staff, training style, players, and parents are the organization. That realization came to us with the competition from the new club. Even though it caused our club to shrink, it helped us. It taught us that our club is not about the owners—nor should it be.

The second story that emphasizes the need to debunk the myth that you are your business is related to Beachfront Buggies and Scooters, another business I started with friends.

We quickly found out our business has many facets, and we are just a small part of its success.

You should have been there the day my neighbor Eric presented the idea to start the business to another neighbor, Joey, and me. Eric owned an electric car. I loved it so much that I

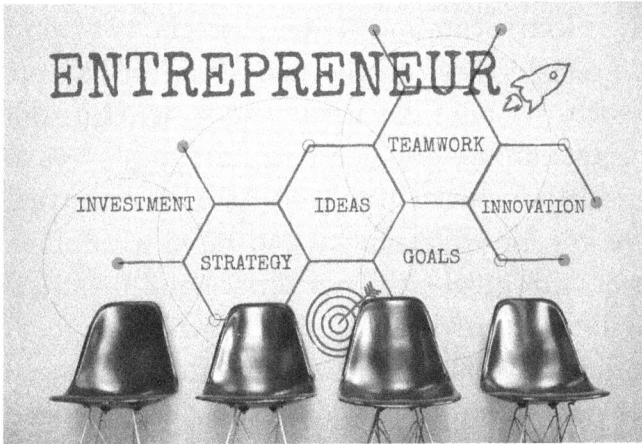

bought one, too. Eric explained that no one on the beach rented out electric cars. In addition, there was only one scooter shop on the beach, and it had an exceptionally low TripAdvisor rating. Eric described this as a fun business, enhancing people's beach experiences, and it could be started for about $75,000, or $25,000 each. Everything could be done by an online booking system, so the shop could be run by a college student or a part-time employee if managed properly by its three genius owners. In other words, we would own the business but not need to be there to supervise in any way. We would be like silent partners.

In October 2018, we bought all the equipment: five electric cars and twelve scooters. We found a great location on the main road of St. Pete Beach. We built the automated system but still needed to hire full- and part-time employees to check the vehicles in and out. As we interviewed, we got incredibly lucky and hired a full-time guy with great customer service and theatrical skills. He previously did walking ghost tours and trolley tours. Our part-time guy had owned a bar/restaurant and a coffee shop and managed several places. Honestly, we really were not looking for such skilled people. We believed the myth that as the owners, *we* were our business. In fact, we thought our automation would allow *anyone* to do the job. Then something happened—we started getting five-star reviews on TripAdvisor, Yelp, and Google.

The immediate success of the business allowed us to shape our goals for it. Automation was running the business, so we decided to open at least two more locations. We felt if each location could make $100,000, we could each add that to our family's income. So, we evaluated where to open our two other locations: Treasure Island and downtown St. Petersburg were selected. Once again, since we felt the owners are the business, the only thing we thought we had to do was find contractors to run each location. We only needed one person per location since we decided to just be open on the weekends until the busy season.

Eight months after our St. Pete Beach location opened and was running smoothly, we opened the Treasure Island location. About three months after that, we opened downtown St. Petersburg. Everything seemed to be going great, and our scalability model was progressing. Then, we found our full-time contractor passed out behind our St. Pete Beach location; he had been drinking on the job, so we had to fire him. This was not a big deal for us because we felt the business could be run by anyone. Instantly, our business started to decline in revenue,

THE MYTH THAT YOU *ARE* YOUR SMALL BUSINESS LED US TO THE CONCLUSION THAT OUR AUTOMATED SYSTEM AND OUR OWNERSHIP WERE THE PROBLEMS.

and our customer-service reviews started to decrease. Simultaneously, we did not see any revenue from the downtown location. In addition, the Treasure Island location was on resort property, and it was unhappy with our staff's unprofessionalism. It started to become apparent that *we* were not the business.

Confronted with these issues at each location, we started to examine the causes. The myth that you *are* your small business led us to the conclusion that our automated system and our ownership were the problems. However, I brought up the observation that all these problems were due to poor management by us as the owners; our staff not implementing great customer service; and not providing the product in an efficient, professional manner. In addition, our staff was not good at troubleshooting problems to make customers happy.

We started to address the situation by hiring a manager, Peter, who was amazing at customer service. Then, we met with all our staff to train them on how to execute great customer service and fix problems; we emphasized professional attire and improved communication. Our staff immediately improved its productivity, professionalism, and customer service. As a result, our host resort at Treasure Island and at the art center downtown were extremely impressed with the improvements. Our revenue returned to what it was before our slump. The customer-service ratings went back up to 4.7 or better. We achieved the goal of successfully running three locations to scale our business. We learned it was a myth that we were our small business. The automation and our ownership were not the business. Our staff was our business. It had direct contact with customers, so it created our brand, provided our service, and was the real X-factor.

Fast-forward to February 2020: We decided to close the downtown location because we understood that quality staff was needed. We could not overextend our great staff to more than two locations. Plus, to provide the best product, we needed all inventory for our beach locations. We decided to use our great staff members and the downtown inventory to provide top-quality service at both beach locations. Treasure Island expanded to seven days a week, and we are excited to see what happens this year.

What is the moral of the story? Your business is not about *you*. It is about the people who have a direct impact on your customers and who represent your brand. My partners and I learned that you need, as Jim Collins said, not only the right people on the bus but in the right seat. Our role is to mentor these people; they are our business.

YOUR BUSINESS IS NOT ABOUT *YOU*. IT IS ABOUT THE PEOPLE WHO HAVE A DIRECT IMPACT ON YOUR CUSTOMERS AND WHO REPRESENT YOUR BRAND.

APPLICATION BOX

1. List three people or positions that are crucial to define your business.

2. List three concepts you can implement to build the culture of the business.

3. Explain how your product or service defines you business.

4. List three things your can do to build relationships with your staff that will enhance customer service.

5. List three strategies that your staff can implement to ensure customer satisfaction.

CHAPTER FIVE

MYTH 3: **THE TREATMENT MYTH**

IT IS EASY TO PROVIDE GREAT CUSTOMER SERVICE

Many make a big mistake believing the myth that it is easy to provide great customer service. People think after they give a customer a product or a service, they did their job. However, there is so much more to customer service than simply providing goods or services. It includes the delivery before, the process of providing it, the communication after they receive their product

THERE IS SO MUCH MORE TO CUSTOMER SERVICE THAN SIMPLY PROVIDING GOODS OR SERVICES.

or service, and their emotions during this whole process. Here are a couple of short stories that will debunk the myth that it is easy to provide great customer service.

In the fall of 2018, my partner Eric and I started Beachfront Buggies and Scooters. At that time, we both had full-time jobs; this was supplemental income for us. However, I ran into an issue at my coaching job when I was told by my athletic director that I would be suspended for two weeks (six games) due to a technical NCAA compliance error I made. Fair enough. So, I walked into the office on Friday to receive my discipline. However, I was blindsided by our human resources director firing me for the mistake. I was in total shock. So, what was supposed to be supplemental income was now needed to help replace wages from my full-time position.

We chose the business for a couple of reasons. First, we saw no one was renting electric cars on the beach. In fact, there was only one rental company on the beach, which primarily offered scooters and bicycles. Second, we both loved customer service and believed enhancing people's experiences on the beach would be easy and rewarding. We knew there would be challenges; neither of us knew the beach market or had experience in the field. Plus, we were starting during the slow season—beach business is mainly from February through August.

Eric and I sat down and defined our business model. We wanted to build a scalable business model with an emphasis on customer service. If we could learn how to run a rental business with phenomenal customer service, we could open four or five locations and achieve our goal of scalability. In quantitative measures, our goals were to reach $150,000 in sales and have a customer-service rating of at least a 4.7 on TripAdvisor, Yelp, and Google.

Since Eric and I were not running the day-to-day operations, we knew we needed to build a culture of customer service, starting with a great manager. In addition, we would need to hire support staff to assist in daily operations. I interviewed many people before finding Peter. Then Peter and I hired Amanda and Aiden. Eric and I met with the staff to expound on the goal of revenue and our customer-service ratings. Our philosophy was that if any customer had an issue with their experience, we would compensate them. Depending on the issue, they would receive a discount, gift certificate, or even a complete refund. In addition, we emphasized it was everyone's job to really connect with every customer through conversation. Employees asked every customer for authentic feedback on Yelp, Google, and TripAdvisor on their experience.

Like any new business, we quickly learned that easy customer service was a myth. One of the biggest problems was our electric cars needed to be plugged in when not being used and could only run twenty miles on a charge. We had to fix the problem by changing our whole fleet from electric to gas golf carts. This change was expensive since we had to sell all the electric carts at a discounted price to unload them quickly. Then, we had to purchase brand new carts and pay to have them made street legal. Each new cart was about $13,000. However, we knew we needed to focus on customer service to make sure the customers' experience was a lifelong memory. The gas carts provided stability and reduced the opportunity of technical issues, which enhanced overall satisfaction.

The second issue we found was that tons of people wanted more adventure than just renting a scooter or golf cart. Hearing that, I came up with the idea of creating a scavenger hunt or guided tour. Eric contacted an app company that assisted him in building this experience. The app company did not charge us to build the scavenger hunts, but they did charge us a fee per user, which we were fine with because it enhanced our customers' experience. He built a twelve-stop scavenger hunt and a self-guided tour. These locations were top places that people needed to see on their trips; some were tourist spots, but others were only known by the locals—so customers got an inside look at some hidden treasures of the area.

These products fit two different customers' desires; scavenger hunts were tailored to people who wanted to try to find the locations themselves, while self-guided tours were for those who did not want to hunt for locations—we gave them addresses. In both cases, they had something to do when they rented our equipment. The great thing was Eric could change the tours whenever he wanted to provide different experiences for return customers.

As 2019 passed by quickly, we constantly focused on customer service and our growing sales. Eric and I had our end-of-the-year meeting in December to examine the business and plan for 2020. Eric is an expert at collecting and crunching data from our online booking system and our customer-service measurement companies. I remember he pulled out the first

paper, and it said total sales were $180,000, which was $30,000 over our goal. Next, he showed me our 4.9 ratings on all customer-service platforms. In fact, we have over one hundred five-star reviews on TripAdvisor, and our new company was number four of all things to do on St. Pete Beach.

In 2020, we opened our second location in Treasure Island, giving Eric the chance to build more hunts and tours. We still receive tons of calls from return customers. Beachfront Buggies and Scooters has found its niche as a great customer service-based business.

What is the moral of the story? It is a myth that customer service is easy. You must overdeliver and know your customers better than they know themselves by building relationships with them and using their authentic feedback.

The other story about customer service is based on a friend of mine who learned about customer service the hard way. In fact, he almost lost everything because he made a common mistake—focusing on revenue instead of relationships. This story will further debunk the myth that it is easy to provide good customer service.

Joey was a young man who graduated from college a couple of years ago. His dad told him if he wanted to make money, he had to own a business. So, Joey started his own title company but found himself in a tough spot. The business was struggling; he almost lost

YOU MUST OVERDELIVER AND KNOW YOUR CUSTOMERS BETTER THAN THEY KNOW THEMSELVES BY BUILDING RELATIONSHIPS WITH THEM AND USING THEIR AUTHENTIC FEEDBACK.

his house and could barely pay the bills. He was forced to collect unemployment and tried to survive as the business failed. On top of that, no one was hiring in his field due to the housing market crash.

Joey was at a crossroads in his life. What was he going to do without a job? Then, he decided to try to start his own business a second time. He met a guy who owned a title company and approached him about being partners in a new venture. The man gave Joey three title files as a test of his competency. Joey knew he had to handle these files as if they were his last clients on Earth.

Joey learned from his previous mistakes that focusing on revenue was not the solution. He knew good customer service was not just closing these files. He had to exceed the needs of each individual client. For example, one of the three clients wanted daily communication, so Joey provided updates at least twice a day. Joey also knew he had to connect with these clients on a personal level; many people could just close files. Joey took one client on a chartered fishing trip and another to a baseball game. He achieved the goal of giving all three clients a great experience and closed their files successfully.

As a result, Joey and his colleague formed a partnership. As they began to grow, they bought other small businesses with established clientele. One owner sold them a fifteen-client title company for $60,000. Joey then made the mistake of focusing on growth again—forgetting the lessons he had learned about the importance of customer service. He did not build relationships or take time to understand these clients' individual needs. Consequently, he lost most of them—and his $60,000 investment. For the next three years, he and his partner focused on avoiding that mistake again. In fact, they bought a ten-client title company in Tampa for $65,000. Shortly after, Joey spent time building relationships with these clients through fishing trips, baseball games, and dinners. With this focus, they grew their business to between forty and fifty clients, producing almost $1 million in gross sales.

Seven years later, in 2019, Joey and his partner had over one hundred clients, two offices, and more than $2 million in gross sales. He went from being a failed business owner to having twelve employees. His main job now is to build relationships with existing clients and acquire new ones.

What is the moral of the story? It is a myth that providing good customer service is easy. In fact, you need to go beyond customer expectations and build relationships. That is how you start and grow a small business.

APPLICATION BOX

1. List three ways you can improve your customers' experience.

2. List three ways you can compensate unhappy customers.

3. List one way to overdeliver what customers expect.

4. Write a review you would like to see about your business.

5. List three ways to focus more on customer service than revenue.

CHAPTER SIX

MYTH 5: **THE HOW MYTH**

HOW YOU SHOULD LOOK AT YOUR BUSINESS

As human beings, it is typically common to focus on problems and weaknesses when we analyze things. This happens in business as well. When starting or growing a small business, many say you need to critically analyze the business's problems and weaknesses—focusing on what is wrong with it. People believe this approach will improve the business model and make it successful. Thinking this is how you should be looking at your business to make it great is another myth of starting or growing a small business. In fact, your critical analysis needs to focus on the positives or strengths of the business. By ignoring this myth, you will improve productivity and enhance the opportunity to be successful.

While owning my businesses, for nineteen years, I maintained my full-time job as a college volleyball coach, which I considered another tough business to run. You may say coaching is not a small business, but I would disagree. I was the CEO; my assistant coaches were vice presidents; and I had an operating budget, staff salary (scholarships), and administrative staff— and we had to provide a successful service. From 2000 to 2003, I was the head coach at a local junior college. In my four years there, we were number-one on the west side of Florida and number two in the state. We won conference titles and went to the national championships all four years.

Then, in the spring of 2004, something happened. I got a phone call to run another "business." A small Division II university offered me the

IN FACT, YOUR CRITICAL ANALYSIS NEEDS TO FOCUS ON THE POSITIVES OR STRENGTHS OF THE BUSINESS.

head volleyball coach position (CEO). This program was historically horrible. Over the previous twenty years, this business had never produced a quality service—that is, a winning season. So, I was faced with a dilemma—stick with a business that had been successful since its start in 1990 or lead a business that had been struggling since its origin in 1980. I like challenges, so I took the position.

As the new CEO of this unsuccessful, small private university's volleyball program, I knew I had to analyze the business and establish short-term goals. These would help me with the primary goal—building a successful volleyball program. So, I did what most people do when confronted with an issue: I looked at the negative characteristics of its service. Some experts estimate that people look at negative aspects four times more than positive ones when confronted with a problem. I wanted to achieve a 180-degree transformation by fixing those negative issues. My business was in the bottom third of the volleyball programs in Florida. I felt our program had to be in the top three out of the nine programs in Florida to accomplish our goal.

In May of 2004, I officially took over the program. Going with the myth that you must use critical analysis to grow the business, I found two major problems that needed to be addressed to be successful. First, we needed better players (staff) in the organization. My old CEO always said, "You can't win the race without the horses." This should have been easy, as we could release the weaker players and recruit new ones to replace them. However, there were two obstacles. We only had a small recruiting budget, and most of this money was tied up in our best players/staff. The recruiting season was basically January through April, so I had missed out on most of the high-quality recruits.

Second, we had one of the lowest operating budgets in the whole state. I was told by the university's administration we needed to fundraise to add to the recruiting and operations budgets. Once again, the timing was an issue. My season started in August, so we could not address this problem immediately.

Since I could not solve my two biggest problems to increase productivity, I had to go against the philosophy of attacking what was wrong. So, I looked at two things we were good at: culture and the staff's willingness to learn and grow. With our culture of positivity, I began to create tasks and workouts that would get the most out of my average talent. This team had never been successful; it lacked confidence, but I knew we could build it—starting with me. I built credibility by explaining how I had taken my previous team to four straight national championships. The staff began to believe in themselves. This helped with their growth curve, too. They were open to learning, but proof of success made them soak up new information. The administration/coaching staff taught them new techniques, how to increase efficiency and to better understand the work atmosphere. This growth continued throughout our 2004 season.

We needed to win our last conference game. At the time, we were 7-8 overall in the tough Sunshine State Conference. If we won our last match, we would finish third, but if we lost, we would move into fifth place. Every competitor in this business was good, so we needed to produce our best service to win this match and reach our goal. The team's positive culture and what it had learned could not be denied that day. We won the match and finished third in the conference which, by our standards, was a successful season.

Fourteen years later, in my last season in 2017, the business had made the biggest turnaround of any in the conference. We won two conference championships, made the NCAA tournament eight out of fourteen seasons, and were identified as a top-three program in the Sunshine State Conference.

The moral of the story? If I had focused on the norm of trying to correct the team's problems, we would not have become a successful "business." Instead, I focused on helping my staff to become great at things it was good at already. It is a myth that you must focus on problems to grow or start a business; you must focus on any positive aspects and improve them first. Then, you can slowly improve your problem areas.

Focusing on problem areas in *critical* analysis is what most people do to create success. However, I took a hard look and made a *positive* analysis to increase productivity. Here is another story

IF I HAD FOCUSED ON THE NORM OF TRYING TO CORRECT THE TEAM'S PROBLEMS, WE WOULD NOT HAVE BECOME A SUCCESSFUL "BUSINESS."

about building on good things instead of major problems.

For the last ten years, I have owned a beach volleyball tournament business called Sunshine State Outdoor Volleyball Association (SSOVA). SSOVA is known as "The first tour for the players and by the players." People found it refreshing that the tour was run by a volleyball player who understood tournaments. I ran tournaments all over the west coast of Florida, from Fort Myers to Clearwater Beach. The volleyball community loved that I provided them with opportunities to play events every month somewhere in Florida.

In 2017, in the eleventh year of the business, my tour experienced a huge slump due to focusing on the wrong age group. Participation for the adult teams dropped by 50 percent, and by 25 percent for the junior teams. I was very frustrated, as tournaments have static costs like beach rental, permitting, setup/teardown, and staffing. Plus, the tournaments' only revenue was from team entry fees, so my income was down about 35 percent. I started to examine my business to decide on a course of action.

I determined one of my two biggest problems was lack of revenue due to low participation, which was directly related to a new tour that just started in St. Petersburg. The other problem was my costs were increasing. Luckily, I learned from an earlier business venture that I needed to focus on our strengths, not problems. So, I realized our tour was organized and valued the player's experience. These strengths came from my connection to the tournaments. I was still a player and understood what players wanted—for tournaments to be well run and cater to them. My goal was to focus on these two strengths and increase my team participation to seventy-five adult teams and one hundred junior teams per event.

I began to implement these two focal points when I ran into a couple of obstacles. The new tour was offering events in the same area at almost half the cost. It used the exceedingly small and inexpensive Gulfport Beach. We used Clearwater Beach, recently named the number-one beach in the US, so it was very pricey. The other obstacle was my new competitor—because we all know people like to check out the shiny new toy.

Since my tour was organized, I went the extra mile to be known as the most organized in Florida. I made sure every event started on time, put time restraints between matches, used a computer app to make the events digital, started playoffs fifteen minutes after pools finished, and awarded prizes immediately after the finals. Only SSOVA did these things, while the new tour was still learning the ropes, which frustrated players.

The other strength we worked on was improving the player experience. Most tournaments did not give out free t-shirts, or if they did, the shirts were extremely low quality. So, we decided to give players free soft t-shirts; basic but very comfortable and great for branding. The players loved these shirts, and they became a great marketing tool for us indirectly. In addition, we enhanced their experience by improving prizes, creating serving games, adding spectator games, announcing all championship matches, playing all championship matches on center court, and implementing a reward system.

At the end of the season, I opened my tournament software to analyze our data. I found great news—we were averaging about one hundred junior teams and one hundred adult teams per event; we had met our junior team goal and exceeded our adult team goal.

In 2019, my business was the official volleyball tour for juniors in the state of Florida. We are currently sponsored by the Florida Region of USA Volleyball. Our player reviews are mostly five stars. We have great participation numbers. We are known as the tour that focuses on creating the best player experience possible. The moral of the story? Focus first on things you do well; it will improve productivity in your business. Then, you can address problems in a timely manner.

APPLICATION BOX

1. Identify your business's top three attributes.

2. List three things most important to your customer.

3. List things that differentiate yourself from your competitors.

4. List ways you can improve on each of your positive attributes.

5. List some problems you need to address after you improve your strengths.

CHAPTER SEVEN

MYTH 6: **THE SPENDING MYTH**

YOU MUST SPEND TONS ON MARKETING

When starting or growing a small business, many agree that marketing is one of the most important parts of your business plan. In fact, Tony Robbins says marketing and customer service are two of the most important aspects of a business. He owns over sixty companies and earned over $6 billion in revenue in 2019, so I trust his opinion.

Since marketing is such a vital part of business success, people feel they must spend a large amount of money on it. For example, television advertising is a major cost for many companies. However, I would say just because marketing is crucial to your business, that does not mean you must spend tons of money on it. You must spend tons on marketing is another myth of starting or growing a small business. In fact, I have been successful by using organic marketing: word-of-mouth, Google and Yelp reviews, and low-cost printed materials. Here are a couple of stories that prove success without spending tons of money on marketing is possible.

My second small business, Tampa United Volleyball Academy, launched in 1997, and I still run it today. My first high school teaching job also involved coaching volleyball. While coaching, I was approached by five girls on my team to start my own club volleyball program. I knew what each player paid to play club volleyball; it could be a profitable business. During this time, I was also running my first business, Tampa Tutoring. However, I told my players if they could get five other girls willing to join, I would start a one-team club. My players were ambitious and found five more players.

The only catch was that in club volleyball, the oldest person on your team sets the age group. Of my five players, one was an eighteen-year-old senior, so we needed to play as an eighteen-and-under team. Most of my team were sixteen-year-olds; people were impressed we could play in the eighteen's division with younger girls.

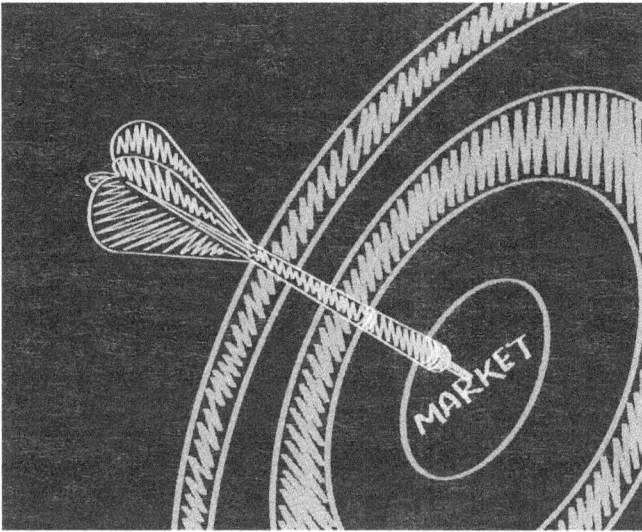

We had a great first year. The team had moderate success, but more importantly, all the players' skill levels improved drastically. I realized this was a business I wanted to pursue. However, I had to get the word out and build interest for people to try out for my club. Would they leave their own current volleyball club to join Club Tampa Volleyball (now Tampa United Volleyball Academy)? I did not have any money for advertising or a marketing plan. The only thing I knew was that I needed at least a four-team club to close Tampa Tutoring to focus on the volleyball club; I needed forty players from eight to eighteen to pay about $3,000 each. My goal was to clear about $60,000, which would be a great supplemental salary for me and a bonus because I loved coaching volleyball more than any job in the world.

It was volleyball season for the fall of 1997, and I had to advertise tryouts at the end of the high school season in mid-November. There were many obstacles to growing this one-team club into four teams. How would I reach the elementary and middle school kids? Plus, how would I get high school players? So, I decided to use the most powerful free marketing tool I had learned from Tampa Tutoring: referrals. I met with my club team and their parents. I had them talk to all their friends, other families, and anyone who had potential athletes. I also held some free clinics at the middle and elementary schools. Finally, I passed out flyers at all my high school volleyball JV and varsity games. Since my teams were good, I felt this was the place to attract competent players.

The season flew by, and the moment of truth came as we did our tryout at the local YMCA in mid-November. We had seventy kids show up. Based on the breakdown of ages and skill development, we made five teams, and my profit margin was $70,000. I exceeded my goal by growing my one-team club into a *five*-team club with some talented athletes. We had teams composed of middle and high school students. So, my low-cost marketing strategy worked, since I acquired high schoolers and younger kids, too. My emphasis on referrals, holding free clinics, and passing out flyers proved to be inexpensive ways to market that worked.

Twenty-one years later, my club is the longest-running in the Tampa Bay area. I had as many as twenty-five teams at one point, and we have sent hundreds of kids to college on scholarships. This business has become my primary income. In addition, it allowed me to run huge tournaments, which produce even more profit than the club itself. Our profit margin for these tournaments is substantial, and we would have never gotten this opportunity to host without running a club.

The moral of the story is that I started and grew a small business through word-of-mouth, free clinics, my high school team's success, and some flyers. All that marketing cost me about $100 in total. In fact, the only marketing my club has done over the last ten years is by word-of-mouth, and we also rely on the power of testimonials; our website lists all the players we have sent to college on scholarships. Consequently, you do not have to spend tons on marketing to start or grow your business. You just need to provide a great product, so people refer others to you and generate powerful testimonials.

The second story debunking the myth that you must spend tons on marketing is when my partners and I started Beachfront Buggies and Scooters. (See chapter 4.) As with many start-ups, we had to buy equipment and get a storefront. In this case, my investment was $25,000, so we wanted to market without a lot of money. How could we get the word out to local St. Pete Beach residents, surrounding area

YOU DO NOT HAVE TO SPEND TONS ON MARKETING TO START OR GROW YOUR BUSINESS. YOU JUST NEED TO PROVIDE A GREAT PRODUCT, SO PEOPLE REFER OTHERS TO YOU AND GENERATE POWERFUL TESTIMONIALS.

residents, and the biggest group of all—tourists? My partner explained we could use technology as our main avenue for exposure. The great thing about using this method was that it was organic and inexpensive.

Most people use the internet to plan their travel. One of the most popular websites, TripAdvisor, posts reviews/testimonials of tourist experiences. Eric said we should let people rent our equipment for free so we could work out the kinks of operating the store. In addition, we could get feedback on what went well and what we needed to improve. This testing ended up being so valuable; we learned tons about our new business. When we went live, almost all our reviews were five stars, and TripAdvisor had done the marketing for us. Yelp and Google reviews soon followed. Our five-star reviews became our primary marketing tool. Since we earned great reviews on all three platforms, people could rely on them and choose us over our competitors.

Next, Eric pointed out that building our website correctly and including the right words would drastically increase traffic to it. I did not really understand search engine optimization (SEO), but like in any business, you let people who are specialists use their strengths. So, Eric designed the website so we could monitor the analytics. We looked at what was clicked on most, by how many users per day, and many other items. Eric also showed us we could run inexpensive ads on Google and other search engines. He set up Groupon deals as well, which increased exposure exponentially.

In addition to technology, we knew personal relationships with local businesses, hotels, and vacation rental companies were especially important; referrals are probably one of the most underrated ways to gain business. Consequently, we made weekly visits to drop off discount coupons, rack cards, and rewards to each establishment.

After the first year was a success, we launched our second location at Treasure Island. This was a no-brainer, as I negotiated free rent at the beach resort in exchange for offering some free rentals for its guests; an exchange of goods or services is a great way to reduce overhead. In addition, you usually raise revenue through additional exposure. Once again, we basically received free marketing from the resort since it wanted its guests to have a great experience.

After six months, we got extremely ambitious and opened the downtown St. Petersburg location. We were not ready for this expansion—due to poor staffing, the location, lack of equipment, and most importantly, not marketing properly— we eventually had to close the store. We quickly found out most sites like TripAdvisor and Yelp do not allow you to have separate reviews for each location; they are all lumped together on the list of things to do. In addition, my partners and I lived on the beach, so building relationships with businesses and hotels were much easier than in downtown.

Currently, Beachfront Buggies and Scooters is number four of all things to do at St. Pete Beach on TripAdvisor. We are the number-one business on Google when you enter *scooters* or *golf carts on St. Pete Beach*, and we were on a morning news channel as a fun things to do at the beach. We are the busiest scooter shop on the beach and have seen many repeat customers. Our Treasure Island location accounts for 30 percent of our revenue, and we are only open

YOU CAN USE TECHNOLOGY, SOCIAL MEDIA, WEBSITES, PERSONAL RELATIONSHIPS, SEO, REWARDS, ADS, COUPONS, AND GROUPON TO MARKET YOUR BUSINESS FOR EXTRAORDINARILY LITTLE MONEY; YOU DO NOT HAVE TO SPEND TONS ON MARKETING.

Thursday through Sunday part of the year. All this marketing only costs about $500 a month.

So, what is the moral of the story? You can use technology, social media, websites, personal relationships, SEO, rewards, ads, coupons, and Groupon to market your business for extraordinarily little money; you do not have to spend tons on marketing.

APPLICATION BOX

1. Identify your ideal customer and three ways to reach them.

2. Identify three inexpensive marketing tools you can use.

3. List three technology tools for your marketing plan.Identify.

4. List three ways to ensure good reviews.

5. Make a list of people and businesses you need to build relationships with to grow referrals.

6. Explain how you will get to know your customers better than they know themselves.

PART III

WHAT'S NEXT? SUSTAINING GROWTH

CHAPTER 8

CREATING A GROWTH CULTURE BASED ON VALUES

N ow that we have debunked the five myths to starting or growing a small business, you are wondering what comes next. Well, to start or grow a small business, you must begin by defining your core values for the business. These values are based on your personal values and what is needed in that industry. You must choose four to six non-negotiable values for you and your business— ones you can explain by telling a story to your staff, managers, and employees. Everyone must carry out these values without exception.

In the spring of 2004 in New Port Richey, Florida (about forty-five minutes north of Tampa), I was the head volleyball coach at a junior college. I had been there for four successful seasons. We made the state finals all four years, won all four conference championships, and appeared in all four national championships. I was Coach of the Year all four years, as well. Then, I received a call from a small private university about thirty minutes away. The athletic director offered me the head volleyball coach position; but its program was last, and arguably the worst, in the conference since its origination in 1980. And the story gets better, as not only would I be going from first to worst, I was offered a salary of $10,000 *less* than my current pay. It seemed like a no-brainer to decline the offer. However, the new offer had one X-factor, which was the university's six core values: excellence, integrity, community, personal development, responsible stewardship, and respect. This immediately attracted me to the coaching position. I was extremely impressed that this university (which is a business, too) spelled out its values to create its mission. Its student motto was, "You will love the person you become." The university's values made me realize coaching was not just about winning volleyball games—it is about living out your values at work and modeling them so your players will adopt them as well. A coach's goal should be to build relationships with the team and develop members into great student-athletes and people.

In 2019, we were one of the top three programs in the conference. We won a couple of conference championships, made the NCAA tournament many times, and I was Coach of the Year a couple of times.

One day, when we were getting ready to ramp up for the preseason, I was called into the athletic director's office. I thought I was going to be suspended for a couple of games as I made a recruiting violation; I paid a player at the university to coach in my volleyball club, which was legal. The problem was, I paid her salary directly to her landlord, a violation circumventing financial aid procedures. This was an honest mistake; I even wrote checks to create a paper trail.

When I walked into the athletic director's office, I saw our human resources director there, too. I thought it was strange to have her there just to suspend me, but I did not know the protocol. Then, my athletic director started reading my termination letter. As you can imagine, I was totally surprised and devastated. I spent the last fifteen years of my career building a program from nothing to a perennial leader. I had never been in trouble and was considered by everyone in the athletic department as a coach who lived out the core values and was an example to new coaches.

For the first couple of months, I was bitter and depressed. Then, one day, I was talking with God, who reminded me even though my error was a mistake, it was still a violation of the

NCAA rules and the university's values code, so I deserved to be terminated. God punched me in the gut, but I needed it! If a business bends on its values, those values are not a central part of the business. This university made the right decision based on the values posted all over campus. I know many universities have allowed a lot worse and did not fire anyone. However, those universities must not embrace strong values.

As of May 2020, I own five small businesses, and each is centered on my core values: impacting others, caring, respect, and service. Interestingly, all five businesses are service businesses. I believe I subconsciously chose these businesses because they embrace my values. At the end of my journey, I want to be remembered as a businessman who lived out his values.

So, what is the moral of the story? To build a successful business, start with your values and build all other aspects around them. If you have partners, employees, or managers in your business, they must execute your values. It is your job to tell them stories about each of your values. My termination was a tough

CRACKING THE START-UP CODE

experience, but hopefully, it will remind you of the importance of values. It reminded me why I chose that university many years before—because I believed in having values.

APPLICATION BOX

1. List four to six core values and why you chose them.

2. List the topic of the story you will use to explain each value you have. (It can be a story about you or someone you know.)

3. Explain how you will evaluate your business and staff to ensure your values are being *lived*.

4. List strategies to improve your values.

CHAPTER 9

INTO THE FUTURE: A PROCESS, NOT AN EVENT

Now that you have your value system in place, you are ready to develop your business plan. Do not stress about making your business plan perfect, as it will change as your business and the environment change. As the great Greek philosopher, Heraclitus, said, "Change is the only constant in life."

In fact, 2020 brought us significant change in the form of the COVID-19 pandemic. As I am writing this book, my businesses are all shut down; they were deemed non-essential.

During the shutdown, my partner Eric and I decided to change our whole business model. Previously, we rented golf carts and scooters in three-hour increments and offered an interactive scavenger hunt or sightseeing tour. As a result of the changes necessitated by the pandemic, we adopted a car rental model where you could do everything online and just pick up the vehicle with the keys in it, returning it and locking it up yourself. We went from three-hour rentals to full-day rentals with social distancing sightseeing tours and scavenger hunts.

There are many benefits to our new model. We only need labor from 9:00 a.m. to 2:00 p.m., and our employees felt safer as they were not in direct contact with customers. In addition, we moved from our first-floor walk-in shop to an upstairs unit, which reduced our rent by two-thirds. Lastly, we made our sightseeing tour and scavenger hunt safer for our customers by calling it "Escape the Crowds." This new business model has dropped our overhead from $10,000 to $4,000 a month—60 percent! More importantly, we built a model that sticks to our core values of caring, respect, impacting others, and service for our employees and customers.

Monday, May 4, 2020, was our first day open with the new model, and it was a huge success. In fact, we made over $6,000 in the first week. Most importantly, all our customers appreciated the modifications we made to protect them and make them feel comfortable.

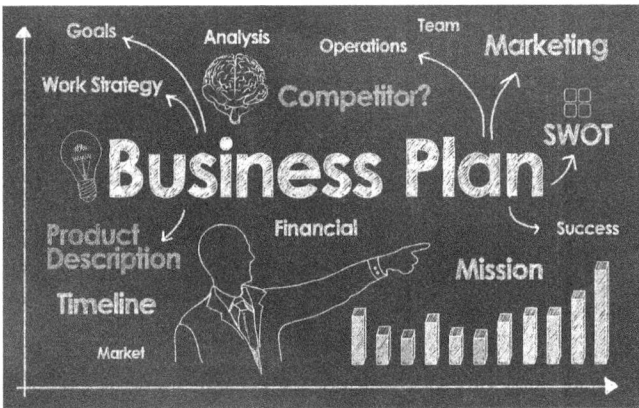

Once again, what is the moral of the story? Even through a crisis like COVID-19, you can endure a changing environment successfully. I am so excited to be writing this chapter. I know you can start a great small business. Too many people talk about the negative sides of doing so. In fact, we hear many misinterpreted statistics. One is small businesses have a 50 to 90 percent chance of failure. The question I have about that statistic is this: how many quit instead of failing?

CRACKING THE START-UP CODE

If you never quit, you never fail! For example, Blogger was a small company that made it easy for people to start their own blogs. In 1999, Evan Williams started his small business, but in 2000, the market crashed, so he fired everyone and was back to running it by himself. Over the next three years, he slowly re-grew his business. He never quit! In its third year, Google bought Blogger for millions of dollars. There are many small business success stories about people who refuse to quit.

I am here to tell you that *you can do it*, but you must follow this basic three-step plan:

- First, you need to create the right mindset. People with negative mindsets fail in business. Avoid the negative influences out there. Usually, people who speak pessimistically about your business are unhappy with their current situation or wish they had the courage to take a chance in business. Remember, none of those five myths should affect your mindset.

- Second, you need to build a value system for your business. Those values will shape your business and allow you to persevere in tough times. Since change is the only constant in life, there *will* be tough times.

- Third, you must develop a solid business plan that allows you to provide your market-dominating advantage. Use your values to create a model your customers want or need. If you always put your values into your business plan, it will be great.

There are numerous benefits to owning a small business; they are different for everyone. Many people have said you should select a job that is based on your passion. However, I tend to agree with author Tom Rath. In his book, *Life's Greatest Question*, he said you should choose a profession that answers this question: "Where can you find your greatest contribution to this world?" I am here to tell you that owning small businesses has allowed me to contribute to the world in many ways.

For example, my tutoring business (Tampa Tutoring) allowed me to help students regain their confidence to improve in school and earn a college degree.

My volleyball club (Tampa United Volleyball Academy) has allowed me to send hundreds of young women to college on volleyball scholarships.

My volleyball tournament business (Tampa United Events) has allowed me to create lifelong memories for young players, coaches, parents, and grandparents.

My golf cart and scooter business (Beachfront Buggies and Scooters) has transformed many vacations into experiences my customers will never forget.

My coaching and speaking business (Sam Cibrone Business Coaching, Inc.) has allowed me to help people start or grow their businesses, affecting the owners, employees, management, and all their families. A small business can have a big impact.

I am so grateful for the opportunity to be on this journey with you. I know you will create a successful small business and provide a great contribution to this world. We are on this journey together, and if there is ever any way I can help you, please reach out to me at www. samcibronebusinesscoaching.com.

Finally, remember an *entrepreneur never quits*. If you do, you will have to deal with that nasty four letter word: *A JOB*. Since you must work anyway, why not work for yourself?

APPENDIX A

ACKNOWLEDGMENTS

I would like to thank some people for their contribution to my life and this book. My wife Jenn has been the biggest supporter of my development of this book. She has always been an encourager and my emotional rock. She allowed me the time and financial freedom to invest in this process. She has been a great business woman and a role model for me, too. She is the best wife a man could ask for, and I thank her from the bottom of my heart.

Also, I would like to thank my editor, Henry DeVries, for his guidance and motivation. He has been an essential part of this book. Henry has always had great input and made me laugh through this process, which has been awesome.

My other mentor for this book has been Dean Minuto. He is an extraordinary person, speaker, author, and father. He has taught me so many lessons, and it has truly been a blessing to be able to call him my next-door neighbor.

Lastly, I would like to thank my friends and family, as without their support, I could not have written this book. Life is all about relationships, and I have been blessed with some of the best people in the world to call family and friends. Thank you for loving me for who I am and pouring into my life.

APPENDIX B

ABOUT THE AUTHOR

Sam Cibrone is a business owner, business coach, and speaker. As a business professional, he has spent the last twenty-three years starting and growing small businesses. He has found five myths that can limit growth or even cause start-ups to fail. Sam has started and grown five successful small businesses and has coached four companies in business growth. He has attended many Small Business Administration courses and has completed the Masterminds course by Tony Robbins and Dean Grazioso. An adjunct professor for over fifteen years, he has taught live training courses on "Starting a Small Business."

Sam lives and works out of St. Pete Beach, Florida, so he can spend his free time playing beach volleyball and traveling with his wife and two children. For more information on Sam as a speaker or for bulk orders of this book, please contact him at sam@cibronebusinesstools.com.

www.ingramcontent.com/pod-product-compliance
Lightning Source LLC
Chambersburg PA
CBHW031947190326
41519CB00007B/694